ISBN 0-590-41737-1

Copyright © 1986 by Jane Miller.

All rights reserved. Published by Scholastic Inc., 730 Broadway, New York, NY 10003, by arrangement with J.M. Dent & Sons Ltd.
12 11 10 9 8 7   3 4/9

Printed in the U.S.A.

For Lizzie and Annie

SEASONS ON THE FARM
Jane Miller

SCHOLASTIC INC.

New York   Toronto   London   Auckland   Sydney

SPRING

It is spring — a new season of the year. On the farm lambing time has begun. Three lambs have just been born in the barn. Big bales of straw shelter them from the cold wind.

In the field the ewe feeds the lambs with milk from her udder.

Patiently, a sheepdog waits to bring back the sheep.

After the chicken has hatched from the egg, the hen will keep it warm under her breast-feathers.

This hen has hatched a goose's egg.
She may not know that her baby
is a gosling and not a chicken!

Goslings cluster around their mother
by a pond. The Canada goose stretches out
a wing to shelter her young.

A mare grazes in the field with her long-legged
foal. These horses work on the farm, pulling
plows and carts.

In the spring, flowers bloom after the winter cold. Primroses grow in the hedgerows; bluebells and red campion in the woods.

Ducks waddle around finding slugs, snails, and insects to eat among the daffodils.

SUMMER

Now it is summer, and time to pick ripe strawberries. How tempting they are.

The Jersey bull with a ring in his nose strides into the yard. He is sometimes as fierce as he looks!

Out in the fields, the sow has given birth to her second litter of piglets this year. Can you see all eight of them sucking her milk? Piglets squeal loudly and greedily at feeding time.

The farmer is cutting grass to make hay to feed his animals.

This grass will be made into silage for the cattle to eat in winter.

In late summer wheat and barley are ripe for harvesting — and threshing. Threshing separates the grain from the straw. On the left, a combine harvester, which cuts and threshes at the same time, is driven back and forth through the fields.

The baler rolls up the straw and ties it into large, round bales.

A truckload of bales is ready to be transported.

You can see the grain pouring out of the spout into the trailer.

AUTUMN

It is autumn and the fruit is ripe in the orchard. The farmer must pick the apples before the frost begins.

A cat's job is to catch the mice that eat the corn.

Many calves are born in the autumn. This Jersey cow is nuzzling her new calf.

After harvesting, the fields are plowed.

Then the tractor pulls a seed-drill through the fields, sowing the seed for next year's crop.

A few farmers still plow their land the old way, using horses instead of a tractor.

Many birds prepare to migrate for the winter. The swallows mass together, perching on the telephone wires before they fly away to warmer countries.

The geese march around the farm.

In the beechwoods the leaves turn red and gold.

WINTER

Finally it is winter. Animals grow shaggy coats to keep themselves warm. The ponies are given hay when the grass is scarce.

A spaniel takes shelter inside the tractor, waiting for the driver.

Seeing the bright sun, a sow grunts and pokes out her snout.

Working on a farm is not always fun. The tractor crunches through mud and ice, carrying straw for the animals' bedding.

Wild ducks have a hard time finding food when the ponds are frozen.

In cold weather, cows live in the barn.

Ponies wait for the snow to thaw
so that they can graze again.

In the woods a hen pheasant searches for food.

A songbird perches on a bud in the garden. He knows that spring is not far away.